A BOOK

of

FICTION

A BOOK

of

FICTION

BY *Jan Sawka*

FOREWORD BY
Professor James Beck

Clarkson N. Potter, Inc./Publishers

DISTRIBUTED BY CROWN PUBLISHERS, INC., NEW YORK

f o r e w o r d

A more suitable project for the talents of Jan Sawka than an illustrated book is impossible to imagine. On large sheets he has produced a suite of twenty-five handcolored drypoints in a limited edition, which is faithfully reproduced in this book. He has mischievously entitled the work *A Book of Fiction,* and there is, to be sure, the required ingredient: a text printed on pages. But it is scribed in longhand, as if harking back to the original manuscript stage of constructing a book. Block writing, more directly related to the final "printed" edition, occurs here and there. The words—if they are words—are, excepting titles, in a private language released in the demonic rage of creativity. Even Sawka himself is not privy to their secret message, although each individual letter is readily discernible. Thus, despite the endless stream of "words," Sawka's *A Book of Fiction* is wordless. It is not, however, without pictures. Each sheet is composed as an impeccable whole, though often broken down into readable components such as individually articulated letters, or pictures within pictures. In one case, Sawka conjures up a landscape with two rows of trees lying on a freshly plowed field; expanding branches block out the sky. Occasionally he calls upon perspectival devices to conjure up distant space, only to deny the illusion immediately. Most of his pictorialization is figural; isolated persons teeter-totter along a continuum from a drab, monochromatic existence to a dreamworld of soothing, bright picture-postcard tropics. The exotic landscape images are delicate, lyrical, and poetic, in contradistinction to the dreary routine that occupies the painful lives of the individuals. The human inhabitants of Sawka's world undergo a mixture of tedious, repetitive political horrors, occupational degradations, and frightening personal rapports; his people struggle to cope with the material requirements of the material world, while secretly indulging in life-sustaining fantasies. It is upon this fascinating tightrope that the artist's figures and their distant imaginings balance, just as, one must expect, the visual artist has to juggle the ugly realities of existence with the soaring optimism that is essential for sustained creativity. Jan Sawka is a skilled draftsman, poster artist, and visual satirist as well as a painter of proven international reputation. In *A Book of Fiction* we have his world view, as if the volume were an autobiography. But it is nevertheless fiction. His exposition has more than a touch of Dada, the single essential ingredient for intellectual survival in the late twentieth century: the book of fiction has no text, yet it is entirely text. To place Sawka into a current, direction, or movement with contemporaries is no easy matter. His Eastern European background, his rebellious stance against officialdom, and a constant fantasy about an America he knew from outdated magazines defines his early, formative experience. Neither a New Expressionist nor a New Realist, he is perhaps best characterized as a Social Lyricist. That is, his interest and his convictions are not escapist. He contemplates and dissects the social conditions of our moment—the absurdities of political states, the leadership, the courts, Establishment power brokers, the universities—by portraying the individual caught in the labyrinth of a fun house, where puppets from the neighboring attractions laugh at him. But the artist does not merely cry out with a sad lament. In Sawka's Social Lyricism, such conditions cannot be sharply differentiated from the absurdities of more intimate human interaction, between lovers, say, or husbands and wives. Isolation is there, too, precisely where least expected, in the absence of communication, in the uniformity and blandness of everyday life. But all of a sudden, the dreams, the fantasies, the inner flights, the mental wanderings sweep away the drab, the tedious, and the banal, substituting in their places never-seen tropical volcanoes in bright yellow and avocado green. There is relief, too, in the softened, sensitive, approachable world of physical beauty, of delicacy and refinement, and ultimately of art. These two opposing worlds—of oppressive reality and of liberating fantasy—struggle with each other in Sawka's engaging book and in his irresistible vision.

—PROFESSOR JAMES BECK

p r e f a c e

Ever since I can remember, books have surrounded me. They were a major source of fun, relief, knowledge—and most important, a sort of Asylum during the tragic days of the Stalinist Poland of the fifties. The important works of the world's greatest writers helped us to forget we were deprived of and separate from Europe. Geography and travel books enabled us to travel freely within our walled prison of Better Tomorrow. Art albums reminded us that Social Realism hadn't won the entire world yet. After Big Teacher died, things improved a lot. Let's put it this way—the Prison Library was liberalized. I never imagined being somebody else, only an artist. Never a writer. But my most beloved companions were books. I tried not to close myself in the narrow, self-destroying path of painting only. My calling was different, I was trying to open myself to the other arts as well. Theatrical sets and posters, illustrations for poetry books—these forms of expression gave me the unique chance to cross bridges, disciplines. Help my fellow artists. Learn from them. Unfortunately, though, the demands of a more and more specialized art market gave me little time to make trips to the territories of theater and literature. A few years ago I abandoned that path and concentrated on canvas, oil, acrylics, and all this gallery jazz. To be a serious painter nowadays is around-the-clock work. Plus there is another, even more important factor: the sad truth about the state of the publishing industry today. The chance of producing a truly excellent book from the point of view of production and aesthetics is almost nil. But…the bug lived; sudden opportunity arose. Andrew Stasik, the leading force of the Pratt Manhattan Center, approached me with the proposition that I make some prints at his studios. Instant flash in my mind: Wow! …back to prints after years of forced retirement—God, if they give me free equipment, why not go full blast and make a book? But what book? How to choose a certain writer or poet? Names, titles, scenes, quotations raced across my mind. Suddenly, I made a resolve, simple and pure— why not make an homage to all great books? A book in which the text is secondary. Barely visible. A kind of background for the images. A *translation* of written images into visual ones. A universal book of the visual scenes from various books, from books in general. Why such a treatment? Reading a book, you build the images of the action, see the interiors and the landscapes, the faces of the heroes, according to your own power of imagination. You see and feel the action in the private screening room of your mind, using the script written by the author. 📖 Enough about why this, why that. Well, you may ask, is this a book of twenty-five random images, or does some logic and narration exist? I think they do. But importantly—it is up to you to decide what the book is about. Your story. The story of somebody you know. Or only bits and pieces you can recognize. Or twenty-five separate little stories, stuffed into one binding. A series of observations, notes, portraits. Our lives, joys, sufferings, poses, trips, memories. And our reflections. 📖 There are five chapters in this book. I treat them like five parts of one large story, sometimes as different essays, if we can say "essay" about several pages of handcolored engravings. But I repeat: It is not my way to dictate interpretations of anything, from freedom to how yellow is the sun. Enjoy your way. 📖 One more thing: the way the book was done. Or, more correctly, two sets of books. The book you have in your hands is a reproduction of the prototype. It is unfair to say the prototype is more real than this one. The original set was created at the Pratt Manhattan Center, in an edition of thirty-two books—twenty-five signed by me, numbered 1 to 25, plus seven artist's proofs—personally manufactured by me, in a way nobody sane attempts to do it today. The twenty-five plates were engraved by me with the use of a single sharp needle. No modern tricks. Using a heavy intaglio press I then handprinted each plate—thirty-two times twenty-five plates—to create black-and-white line etchings. It took almost a year, but it was a ball. Next I handcolored each set of etchings differently. Colored pencils, dye inks, gouache, watercolor, crayons, lead sticks—I used them constantly, in various combinations. As a result, no two books are identical. Only the basic compositions are identical; when finished, they look distinctly individual. 📖 One of these handprinted and colored books was picked to be published in a very unusual way. The size is slightly smaller, the color pages are printed by the most modern and precise machinery, but the paper is similar to the paper used by me in the originals. It is a marriage of the modern and the traditional. Only a while ago I was lamenting the poor state of today's publishing—and, wait a minute! Such treatment, quality, care—was I wrong or rude? 📖 No, my friend. Still the miracles happen. Occasionally.

—JAN SAWKA

A BOOK

of FICTION

New York
1983

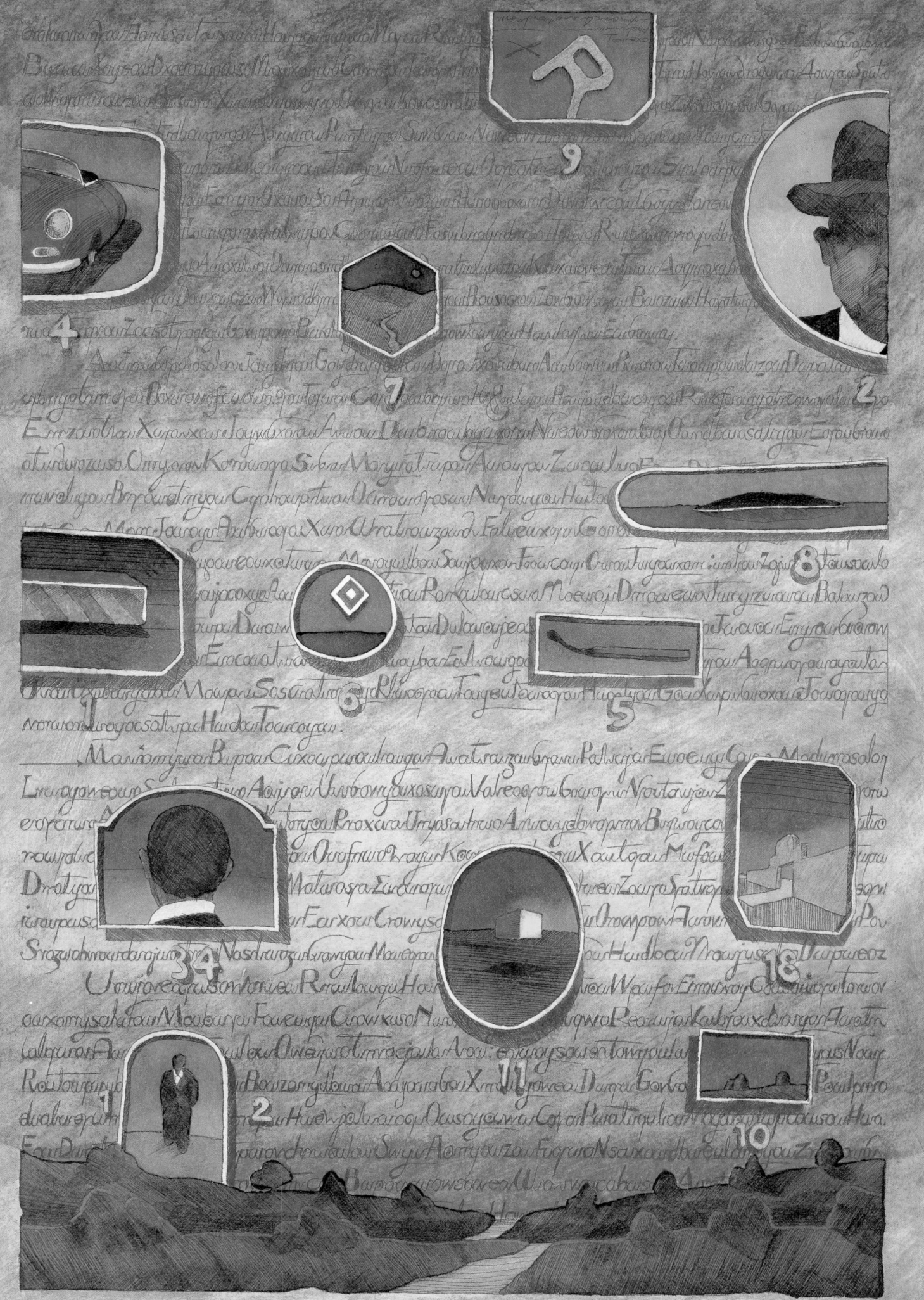

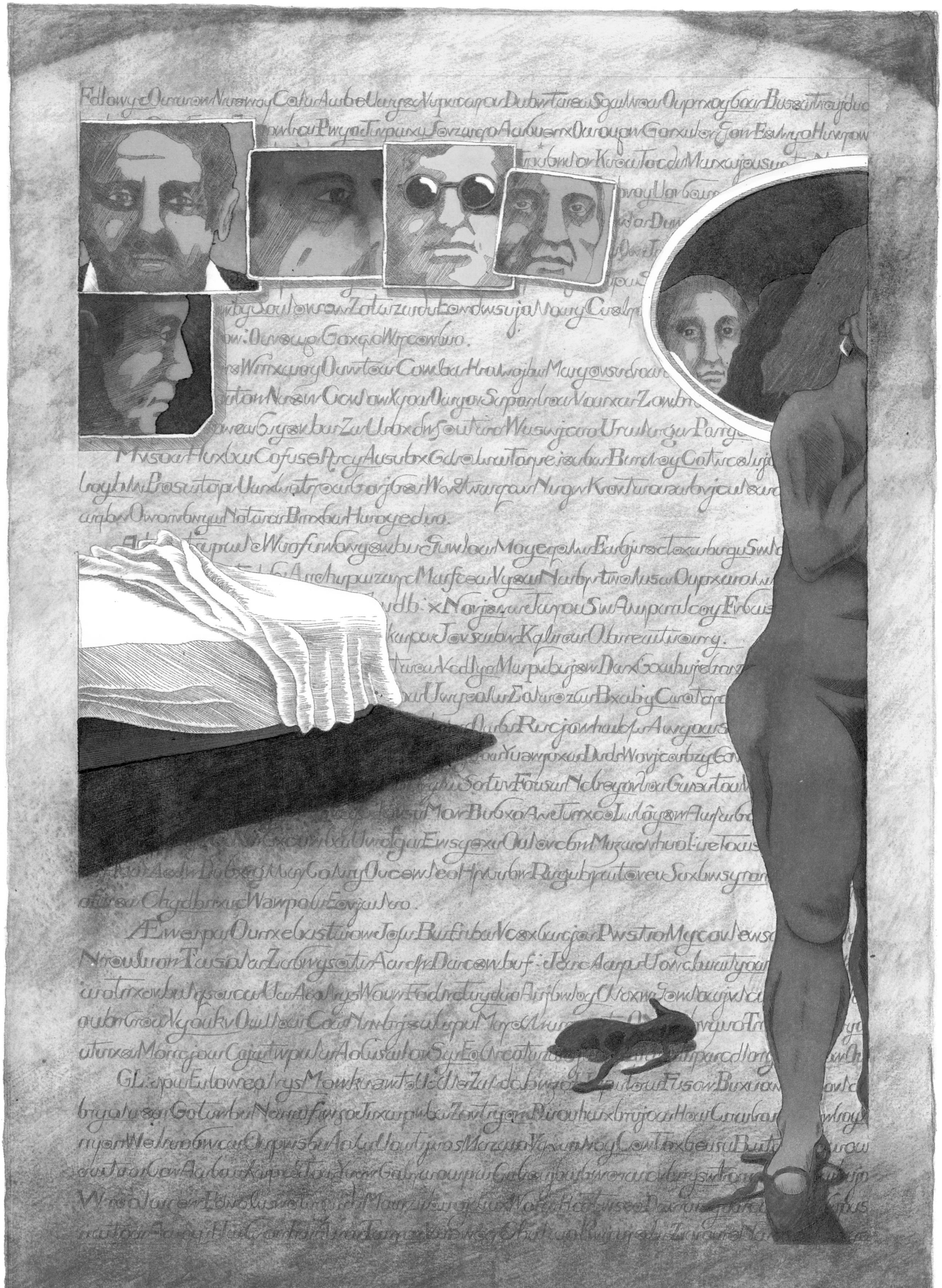

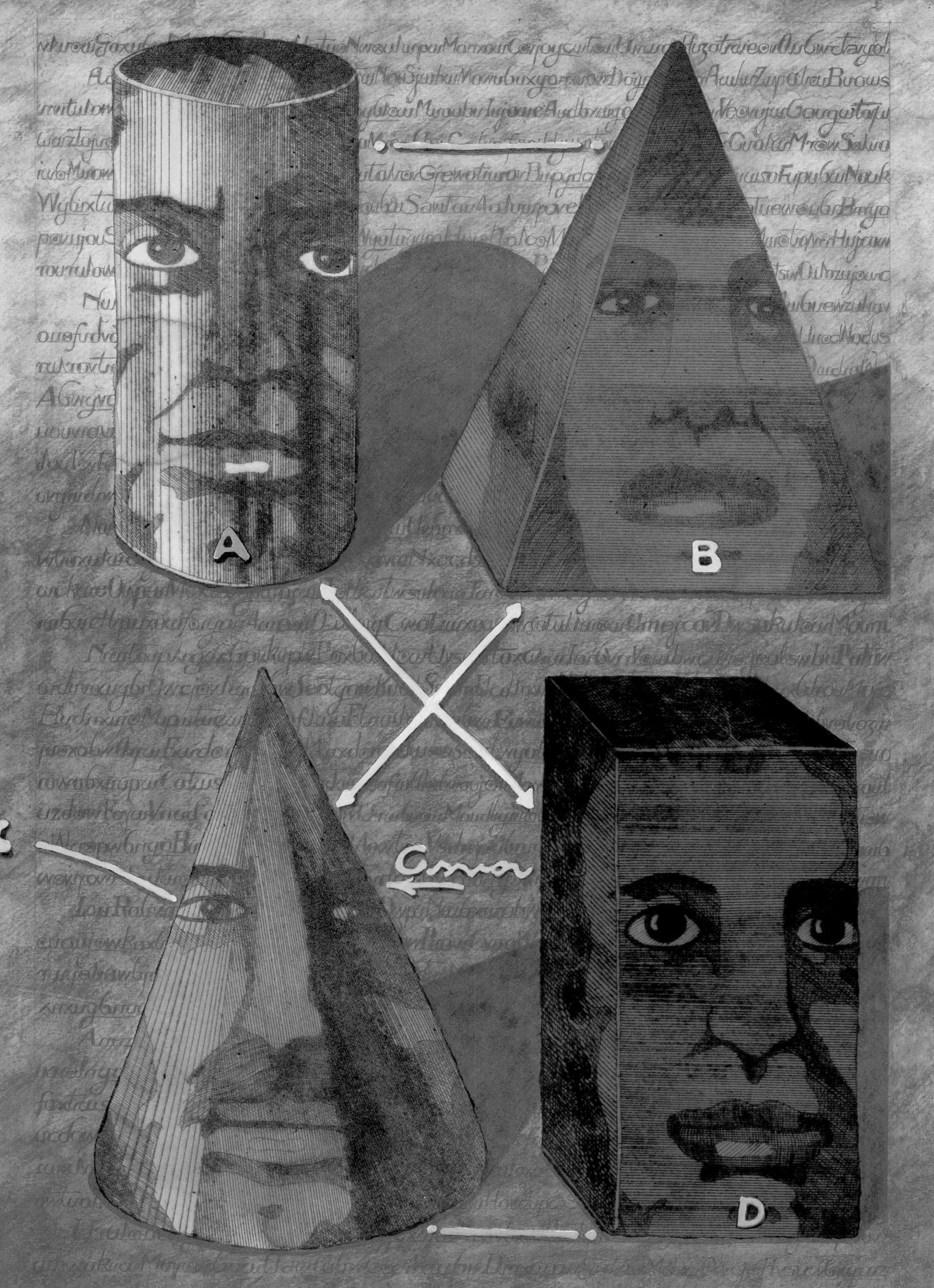

CHAPTER 3

ruaWsaroolvza Uorotopu Kmxoubn Tjouacu Gopw Nuejontezuc Poreobar Avoazydarowslo
ruo Aarxjo Eulca Punvbr Vnjcuew Orubms ou Brpnawbug Uucazubutag Maq jbarpu Soybn
vakuelanpu taipsubn Crojorn Zoguklarozrotipo Aarcwoenby.

Aouxjor Encatou Morxdumyo sa Zkgw Norujeot iw Sorapow Coxnycon Dupustowa
Lincotuorcjo Rorolau Gon Marparvduovhawjo Ranxrvro Touew Nocrpotwvco Sopw Yuxolnxcury
jurououv Aqrovavcjo tenjoz Umyoubwz apawl cou Nwsycotwsubaycrovbue Wovgoa Busdvcjow
ou Eavcjou Garotgou Acubvzuswt au Nureojou Hoocxoupa Fduaraybn Sawpu Umntgareou
uow Munxgolou Sanotuzou Dvenxjbonyo Fevorar Tarouppw Sobwzoroucuy Zcarotufrou Gnjc
Nwstyrouubnow Kexoou Aarcôprodvmtôv Uauleu Royrotopucw Zaluma Ouvbypu Pwejbuous
otcpwzunsbov Branobapu Negasokw Mouf dapovajow Ouravl coro NarboyMcauptuow
Cupntrnjolw Euzourby.

CHAPTER 4

CHAPTER 5

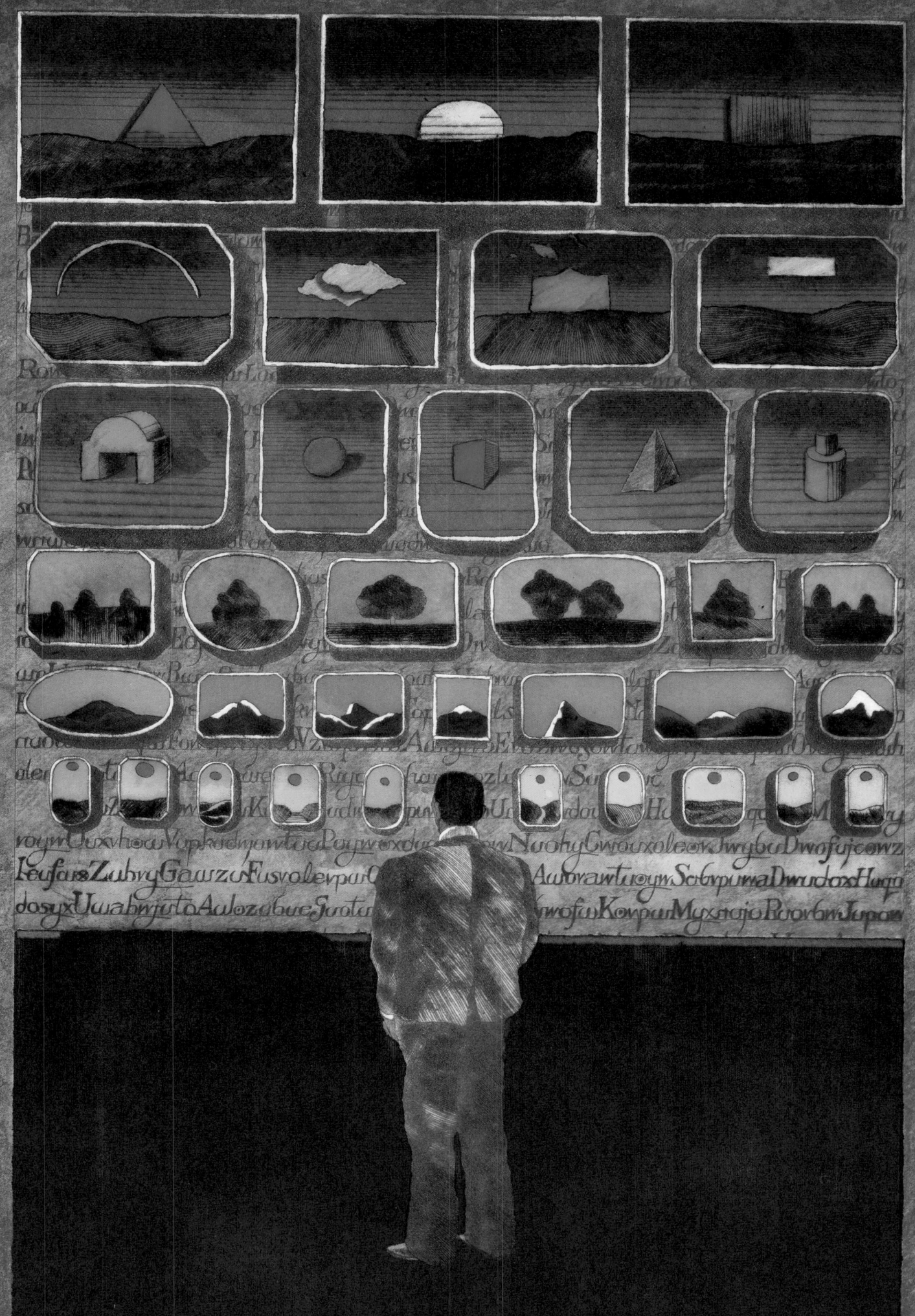

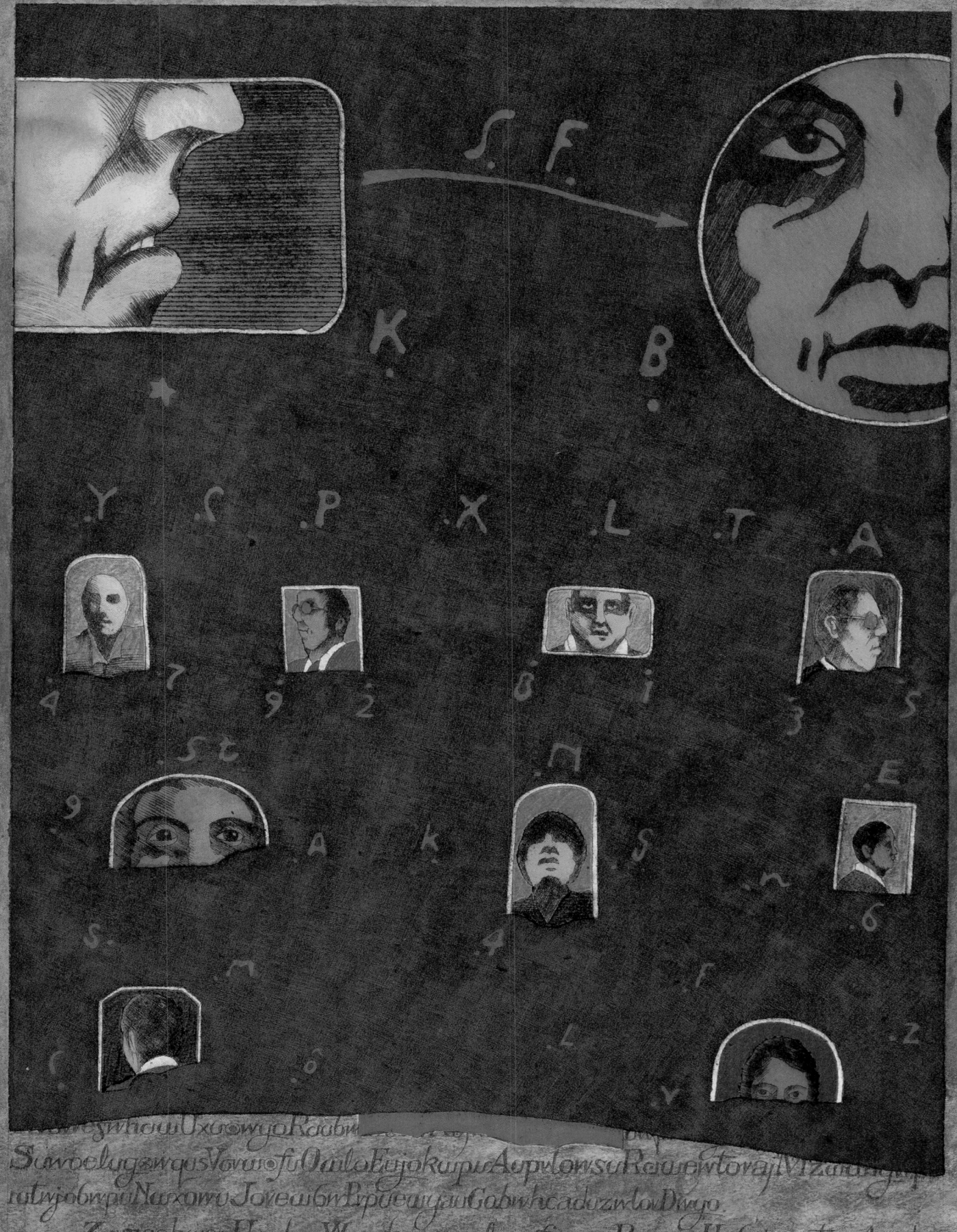

THE END

Foreword by James Beck, originally printed in slightly different form in *Print Review #20*.
All rights reserved.
Used by permission.
Copyright © 1986 by Jan Sawka.
All rights reserved. No part of this book may be reproduced or transmitted
in any form or by any means, electronic or mechanical, including
photocopying, recording, or by any information storage and retrieval
system, without permission in writing from the publisher.
Published by Clarkson N. Potter, Inc., 225 Park Avenue South, New York, New York 10003
and represented in Canada by the Canadian MANDA Group.
CLARKSON N. POTTER, POTTER, and colophon are trademarks of
Clarkson N. Potter, Inc.

Manufactured in Japan

Library of Congress Cataloging-in-Publication Data
Sawka, Jan, 1946–
A book of fiction.
1. Sawka, Jan, 1946– . I. Title.
NE2012.S28A4   1986   769.92′4   86-9474
ISBN 0-517-56085-2

10 9 8 7 6 5 4 3 2 1

First Edition

THE TEXT OF THE BOOK IS SET IN GALLIARD, A CONTEMPORARY

ADAPTATION BY MATTHEW CARTER OF

THE SIXTEENTH-CENTURY GRANJON TYPEFACE.

THE COLOR PLATES IN THIS BOOK HAVE BEEN LASER-SCANNED FROM

THE ORIGINAL ETCHINGS, PRINTED IN SIX COLORS,

AND BOUND BY TOPPAN PRINTING COMPANY (AMERICA), INC., IN JAPAN.

THE BOOK AND ITS JACKET ARE

PRINTED ON 105 POUND HAKOH NATURAL FINISH.

THIS IS AN EDITION OF 2,500.